ISBN: 9781314491890

Published by:
HardPress Publishing
8345 NW 66TH ST #2561
MIAMI FL 33166-2626

Email: info@hardpress.net
Web: http://www.hardpress.net

SONNETS AND OTHER POEMS

Digitized by the Internet Archive
in 2007 with funding from
Microsoft Corporation

http://www.archive.org/details/sonnetsothervers00santrich

FOUR HUNDRED AND FIFTY COPIES
OF THIS BOOK HAVE BEEN
PRINTED ON SMALL
PAPER

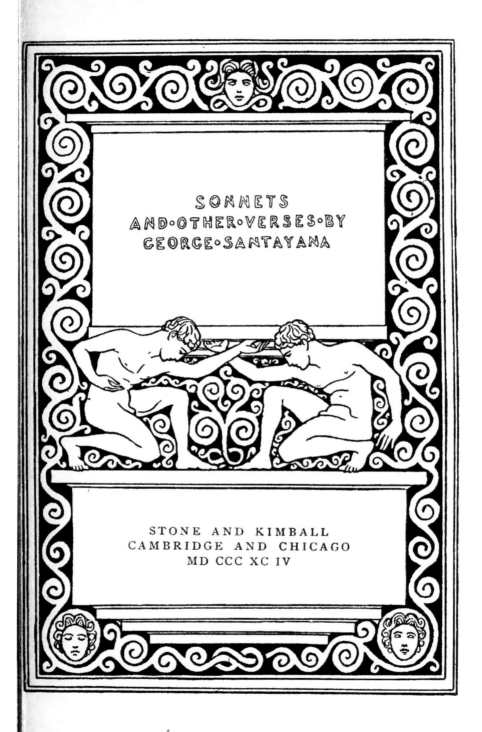

COPYRIGHT
M · D · CCC · XC · IV
BY
STONE & KIMBALL

SONNETS

SONNETS

I

I sought on earth a garden of delight,
Or island altar to the Sea and Air,
Where gentle music were accounted prayer,
And reason, veiled, performed the happy rite.
My sad youth worshipped at the piteous height
Where God vouchsafed the death of man to share;
His love made mortal sorrow light to bear,
But his deep wounds put joy to shamèd flight.
And though his arms, outstretched upon the tree,
Were beautiful, and pleaded my embrace,
My sins were loth to look upon his face.
So came I down from Golgotha to thee,
Eternal Mother; let the sun and sea
Heal me, and keep me in thy dwelling-place.

II

Slow and reluctant was the long descent,
With many farewell pious looks behind,
And dumb misgivings where the path might wind,
And questionings of nature, as I went.
The greener branches that above me bent,
The broadening valleys, quieted my mind,
To the fair reasons of the Spring inclined
And to the Summer's tender argument.
But sometimes, as revolving night descended,
And in my childish heart the new song ended,
I lay down, full of longing, on the steep;
And, haunting still the lonely way I wended,
Into my dreams the ancient sorrow blended,
And with these holy echoes charmed my sleep.

III

O WORLD, thou choosest not the better part!
It is not wisdom to be only wise,
And on the inward vision close the eyes,
But it is wisdom to believe the heart.
Columbus found a world, and had no chart,
Save one that faith deciphered in the skies;
To trust the soul's invincible surmise
Was all his science and his only art.
Our knowledge is a torch of smoky pine
That lights the pathway but one step ahead
Across a void of mystery and dread.
Bid, then, the tender light of faith to shine
By which alone the mortal heart is led
Unto the thinking of the thought divine.

IV

I would I had been born in nature's day,
When man was in the world a wide-eyed boy,
And clouds of sorrow crossed his sky of joy
To scatter dewdrops on the buds of May.
Then could he work and love and fight and pray,
Nor heartsick grow in fortune's long employ.
Mighty to build and ruthless to destroy
He lived, while maskèd death unquestioned lay.
Now ponder we the ruins of the years,
And groan beneath the weight of boasted gain;
No unsung bacchanal can charm our ears
And lead our dances to the woodland fane,
No hope of heaven sweeten our few tears
And hush the importunity of pain.

V

Dreamt I to-day the dream of yesternight,
Sleep ever feigning one evolving theme, —
Of my two lives which should I call the dream?
Which action vanity? which vision sight?
Some greater waking must pronounce aright,
If aught abideth of the things that seem,
And with both currents swell the flooded stream
Into an ocean infinite of light.
Even such a dream I dream, and know full well
My waking passeth like a midnight spell,
But know not if my dreaming breaketh through
Into the deeps of heaven and of hell.
I know but this of all I would I knew:
Truth is a dream, unless my dream is true.

VI

Love not as do the flesh-imprisoned men
Whose dreams are of a bitter bought caress,
Or even of a maiden's tenderness
Whom they love only that she loves again.
For it is but thyself thou lovest then,
Or what thy thoughts would glory to possess;
But love thou nothing thou wouldst love the less
If henceforth ever hidden from thy ken.
Love but the formless and eternal Whole
From whose effulgence one unheeded ray
Breaks on this prism of dissolving clay
Into the flickering colours of thy soul.
These flash and vanish; bid them not to stay,
For wisdom brightens as they fade away.

VII

I would I might forget that I am I,
And break the heavy chain that binds me fast,
Whose links about myself my deeds have cast.
What in the body's tomb doth buried lie
Is boundless; 't is the spirit of the sky,
Lord of the future, guardian of the past,
And soon must forth, to know his own at last.
In his large life to live, I fain would die.
Happy the dumb beast, hungering for food,
But calling not his suffering his own;
Blessèd the angel, gazing on all good,
But knowing not he sits upon a throne;
Wretched the mortal, pondering his mood,
And doomed to know his aching heart alone.

VIII

O MARTYRED Spirit of this helpless Whole,
Who dost by pain for tyranny atone,
And in the star, the atom, and the stone,
Purgest the primal guilt, and in the soul;
Rich but in grief, thou dost thy wealth unroll,
And givest of thy substance to thine own,
Mingling the love, the laughter, and the groan
In the large hollow of the heaven's bowl.
Fill full my cup; the dregs and honeyed brim
I take from thy just hand, more worthy love
For sweetening not the draught for me or him.
What in myself I am, that let me prove;
Relent not for my feeble prayer, nor dim
The burning of thine altar for my hymn.

IX

Have patience; it is fit that in this wise
The spirit purge away its proper dross.
No endless fever doth thy watches toss,
For by excess of evil, evil dies.
Soon shall the faint world melt before thine eyes,
And, all life's losses cancelled by life's loss,
Thou shalt lay down all burdens on thy cross,
And be that day with God in Paradise.
Have patience; for a long eternity
No summons woke thee from thy happy sleep;
For love of God one vigil thou canst keep
And add thy drop of sorrow to the sea.
Having known grief, all will be well with thee,
Ay, and thy second slumber will be deep.

X

Have I the heart to wander on the earth,
So patient in her everlasting course,
Seeking no prize, but bowing to the force
That gives direction and hath given birth?
Rain tears, sweet Pity, to refresh my dearth,
And plough my sterile bosom, sharp Remorse,
That I grow sick and curse my being's source
If haply one day passes lacking mirth.
Doth the sun therefore burn, that I may bask?
Or do the tirèd earth and tireless sea,
That toil not for their pleasure, toil for me?
Amid the world's long striving, wherefore ask
What reasons were, or what rewards shall be?
The covenant God gave us is a task.

XI

Deem not, because you see me in the press
Of this world's children run my fated race,
That I blaspheme against a proffered grace,
Or leave unlearned the love of holiness.
I honour not that sanctity the less
Whose aureole illumines not my face,
But dare not tread the secret, holy place
To which the priest and prophet have access.
For some are born to be beatified
By anguish, and by grievous penance done;
And some, to furnish forth the age's pride,
And to be praised of men beneath the sun;
And some are born to stand perplexed aside
From so much sorrow — of whom I am one.

XII

Mightier storms than this are brewed on earth
That pricks the crystal lake with summer showers.
The past hath treasure of sublimer hours,
And God is witness to their changeless worth.
Big is the future with portentous birth
Of battles numberless, and nature's powers
Outdo my dreams of beauty in the flowers,
And top my revels with the demons' mirth.
But thou, glad river that hast reached the plain,
Scarce wak'st the rushes to a slumberous sigh.
The mountains sleep behind thee, and the main
Awaits thee, lulling an eternal pain
With patience; nor doth Phœbe, throned on high,
The mirror of thy placid heart disdain.

XIII

Sweet are the days we wander with no hope
Along life's labyrinthine trodden way,
With no impatience at the steep's delay,
Nor sorrow at the swift-descended slope.
Why this inane curiosity to grope
In the dim dust for gems' unmeaning ray?
Why this proud piety, that dares to pray
For a world wider than the heaven's cope?
Farewell, my burden! No more will I bear
The foolish load of my fond faith's despair,
But trip the idle race with careless feet.
The crown of olive let another wear;
It is my crown to mock the runner's heat
With gentle wonder and with laughter sweet.

XIV

There may be chaos still around the world,
This little world that in my thinking lies;
For mine own bosom is the paradise
Where all my life's fair visions are unfurled.
Within my nature's shell I slumber curled,
Unmindful of the changing outer skies,
Where now, perchance, some new-born Eros flies,
Or some old Cronos from his throne is hurled.
I heed them not; or if the subtle night
Haunt me with deities I never saw,
I soon mine eyelid's drowsy curtain draw
To hide their myriad faces from my sight.
They threat in vain; the whirlwind cannot awe
A happy snow-flake dancing in the flaw.

XV

A wall, a wall around my garden rear,
And hedge me in from the disconsolate hills;
Give me but one of all the mountain rills,
Enough of ocean in its voice I hear.
Come no profane insatiate mortal near
With the contagion of his passionate ills;
The smoke of battle all the valleys fills,
Let the eternal sunlight greet me here.
This spot is sacred to the deeper soul
And to the piety that mocks no more.
In nature's inmost heart is no uproar,
None in this shrine; in peace the heavens roll,
In peace the slow tides pulse from shore to shore,
And ancient quiet broods from pole to pole.

XVI

A THOUSAND beauties that have never been
Haunt me with hope and tempt me to pursue;
The gods, methinks, dwell just behind the blue;
The satyrs at my coming fled the green.
The flitting shadows of the grove between
The dryads' eyes were winking, and I knew
The wings of sacred Eros as he flew
And left me to the love of things not seen.
'T is a sad love, like an eternal prayer,
And knows no keen delight, no faint surcease.
Yet from the seasons hath the earth increase,
And heaven shines as if the gods were there.
Had Dian passed there could no deeper peace
Embalm the purple stretches of the air.

XVII

Gone is the time when in the teeth of fate
I flung the challenge of the spirit's right;
The child, the dreamer of that visioned night,
Woke, and was humbled unto man's estate.
A slave I am; on sun and moon I wait,
Who heed not that I live upon their light.
Me they despise, but are themselves so bright
They flood my heart with love, and quench my hate.
O beauty, quelling chaos! mighty worth
That didst the love of being first inspire,
We do thee homage both in death and birth.
Thirsting for thee, we die in thy great dearth,
Or borrow breath of infinite desire
To chase thine image through the haunted earth.

XVIII

Blaspheme not love, ye lovers, nor dispraise
The wise divinity that makes you blind,
Sealing the eyes, but showing to the mind
The high perfection from which nature strays.
For love is God, and in unfathomed ways
Brings forth the beauty for which fancy pined.
I loved, and lost my love among mankind;
But I have found it after many days.
Oh, trust in God, and banish rash despair,
That, feigning evil, is itself the curse!
My angel is come back, more sad and fair,
And witness to the truth of love I bear,
With too much rapture for this sacred verse,
At the exceeding answer to my prayer.

XIX

Above the battlements of heaven rise
The glittering domes of the gods' golden dwelling,
Whence, like a constellation, passion-quelling,
The truth of all things feeds immortal eyes.
There all forgotten dreams of paradise
From the deep caves of memory upwelling,
All tender joys beyond our dim foretelling
Are ever bright beneath the flooded skies.
There we live o'er, amid angelic powers,
Our lives without remorse, as if not ours,
And others' lives with love, as if our own;
For we behold, from those eternal towers,
The deathless beauty of all wingèd hours,
And have our being in their truth alone.

XX

These strewn thoughts, by the mountain pathway sprung,
I conned for comfort, till I ceased to grieve,
And with these flowering thorns I dare to weave
The crown, great Mother, on thine altar hung.
Teach thou a larger speech to my loosed tongue,
And to mine opened eyes thy secrets give,
That in thy perfect love I learn to live,
And in thine immortality be young.
The soul is not on earth an alien thing
That hath her life's rich sources otherwhere;
She is a parcel of the sacred air.
She takes her being from the breath of Spring,
The glance of Phœbus is her fount of light,
And her long sleep a draught of primal night.

ON A VOLUME OF SCHOLASTIC PHILOSOPHY

What chilly cloister or what lattice dim
Cast painted light upon this careful page?
What thought compulsive held the patient sage
Till sound of matin bell or evening hymn?
Did visions of the Heavenly Lover swim
Before his eyes in youth, or did stern rage
Against rash heresy keep green his age?
Had he seen God, to write so much of Him?
Gone is that irrecoverable mind
With all its phantoms, senseless to mankind
As a dream's trouble or the speech of birds.
The breath that stirred his lips he soon resigned
To windy chaos, and we only find
The garnered husks of his disusèd words.

ON THE DEATH OF A METAPHYSICIAN

Unhappy dreamer, who outwinged in flight
The pleasant region of the things I love,
And soared beyond the sunshine, and above
The golden cornfields and the dear and bright
Warmth of the hearth, — blasphemer of delight,
Was your proud bosom not at peace with Jove,
That you sought, thankless for his guarded grove,
The empty horror of abysmal night?
Ah, the thin air is cold above the moon!
I stood and saw you fall, befooled in death,
As, in your numbèd spirit's fatal swoon,
You cried you were a god, or were to be;
I heard with feeble moan your boastful breath
Bubble from depths of the Icarian sea.

ON A PIECE OF TAPESTRY

Hold high the woof, dear friends, that we may see
The cunning mixture of its colours rare.
Nothing in nature purposely is fair, —
Her mingled beauties never quite agree;
But here all vivid dyes that garish be,
To that tint mellowed which the sense will bear,
Glow, and not wound the eye that, resting there,
Lingers to feed its gentle ecstasy.
Crimson and purple and all hues of wine,
Saffron and russet, brown and sober green
Are rich the shadowy depths of blue between;
While silver threads with golden intertwine,
To catch the glimmer of a fickle sheen, —
All the long labour of some captive queen.

THE POWER OF ART

Not human art, but living gods alone
Can fashion beauties that by changing live, —
Her buds to spring, his fruits to autumn give,
To earth her fountains in her heart of stone;
But these in their begetting are o'erthrown,
Nor may the sentenced minutes find reprieve;
And summer in the blush of joy must grieve
To shed his flaunting crown of petals blown.
We to our works may not impart our breath,
Nor them with shifting light of life array;
We show but what one happy moment saith;
Yet may our hands immortalize the day
When life was sweet, and save from utter death
The sacred past that should not pass away.

GABRIEL

I know thou art a man, thou hast his mould;
Thy wings are fancy and a poet's lie,
Thy halo but the dimness of his eye,
And thy fair chivalry a legend old.
Yet I mistrust the truth, and partly hold
Thou art a herald of the upper sky,
Where all the truth yet lives that seemed to die,
And love is never faint nor virtue cold.
I still would see thee spotless, fervent, calm,
With heaven in thine eyes, and with the mild
White lily in one hand, in one the palm,
Bringing the world that rapture undefiled
Which Mary knew, when, answering with a psalm
Thine *Ave*, she conceived her holy Child.

TO W. P.

I

Calm was the sea to which your course you kept,
Oh, how much calmer than all southern seas!
Many your nameless mates, whom the keen breeze
Wafted from mothers that of old have wept.
All souls of children taken as they slept
Are your companions, partners of your ease,
And the green souls of all these autumn trees
Are with you through the silent spaces swept.
Your virgin body gave its gentle breath
Untainted to the gods. Why should we grieve,
But that we merit not your holy death?
We shall not loiter long, your friends and I;
Living you made it goodlier to live,
Dead you will make it easier to die.

II

With you a part of me hath passed away;
For in the peopled forest of my mind
A tree made leafless by this wintry wind
Shall never don again its green array.
Chapel and fireside, country road and bay,
Have something of their friendliness resigned;
Another, if I would, I could not find,
And I am grown much older in a day.
But yet I treasure in my memory
Your gift of charity, your mellow ease,
And the dear honour of your amity;
For these once mine, my life is rich with these.
And I scarce know which part may greater be, -
What I keep of you, or you rob from me.

III

Your bark lies anchored in the peaceful bight
Until a kinder wind unfurl her sail;
Your docile spirit, wingèd by this gale,
Hath at the dawning fled into the light.
And I half know why heaven deemed it right
Your youth, and this my joy in youth, should fail;
God hath them still, for ever they avail,
Eternity hath borrowed that delight.
For long ago I taught my thoughts to run
Where all the great things live that lived of yore,
And in eternal quiet float and soar;
There all my loves are gathered into one,
Where change is not, nor parting any more,
Nor revolution of the moon and sun.

IV

In my deep heart these chimes would still have rung
To toll your passing, had you not been dead;
For time a sadder mask than death may spread
Over the face that ever should be young.
The bough that falls with all its trophies hung
Falls not too soon, but lays its flower-crowned head
Most royal in the dust, with no leaf shed
Unhallowed or unchiselled or unsung.
And though the after world will never hear
The happy name of one so gently true,
Nor chronicles write large this fatal year,
Yet we who loved you, though we be but few,
Keep you in whatsoever things are good, and rear
In our weak virtues monuments to you.

ODES

ODES

I

WHAT god will choose me from this labouring nation
To worship him afar, with inward gladness,
At sunset and at sunrise, in some Persian
      Garden of roses;

Or under the full moon, in rapturous silence,
Charmed by the trickling fountain, and the moaning
Of the death-hallowed cypress, and the myrtle
      Hallowed by Venus?

O for a chamber in an eastern tower,
Spacious and empty, roofed in odorous cedar,
A silken soft divan, a woven carpet
      Rich, many-coloured;

A jug that, poised on her firm head, a negress
Fetched from the well; a window to the ocean,
Lest of the stormy world too deep seclusion
      Make me forgetful!

Thence I might watch the vessel-bearing waters
Beat the slow pulses of the life eternal,
Bringing of nature's universal travail
      Infinite echoes;

And there at even I might stand and listen
To thrum of distant lutes and dying voices
Chanting the ditty an Arabian captive
      Sang to Darius.

So would I dream awhile, and ease a little
The soul long stifled and the straitened spirit,
Tasting new pleasures in a far-off country
      Sacred to beauty.

II

My heart rebels against my generation,
That talks of freedom and is slave to riches,
And, toiling 'neath each day's ignoble burden,
    Boasts of the morrow.

No space for noonday rest or midnight watches,
No purest joy of breathing under heaven!
Wretched themselves, they heap, to make them happy,
    Many possessions.

But thou, O silent Mother, wise, immortal,
To whom our toil is laughter, — take, divine one,
This vanity away, and to thy lover
    Give what is needful: —

A staunch heart, nobly calm, averse to evil,
The windy sky for breath, the sea, the mountain,
A well-born, gentle friend, his spirit's brother,
        Ever beside him.

What would you gain, ye seekers, with your striving,
Or what vast Babel raise you on your shoulders?
You multiply distresses, and your children
        Surely will curse you.

O leave them rather friendlier gods, and fairer
Orchards and temples, and a freer bosom!
What better comfort have we, or what other
        Profit in living,

Than to feed, sobered by the truth of Nature,
Awhile upon her bounty and her beauty,
And hand her torch of gladness to the ages
        Following after?

She hath not made us, like her other children,
Merely for peopling of her spacious kingdoms,
Beasts of the wild, or insects of the summer,
        Breeding and dying,

But also that we might, half knowing, worship
The deathless beauty of her guiding vision,
And learn to love, in all things mortal, only
        What is eternal.

III

Gathering the echoes of forgotten wisdom,
And mastered by a proud, adventurous purpose,
Columbus sought the golden shores of India
    Opposite Europe.

He gave the world another world, and ruin
Brought upon blameless, river-loving nations,
Cursed Spain with barren gold, and made the Andes
    Fiefs of Saint Peter;

While in the cheerless North the thrifty Saxon
Planted his corn, and, narrowing his bosom,
Made covenant with God, and by keen virtue
    Trebled his riches.

What venture hast thou left us, bold Columbus?
What honour left thy brothers, brave Magellan?
Daily the children of the rich for pastime
    Circle the planet.

And what good comes to us of all your dangers?
A smaller earth and smaller hope of heaven.
Ye have but cheapened gold, and, measuring ocean,
    Counted the islands.

No Ponce de Leon shall drink in fountains,
On any flowering Easter, youth eternal;
No Cortes look upon another ocean;
    No Alexander

Found in the Orient dim a boundless kingdom,
And, clothing his Greek strength in barbarous
    splendour,
Build by the sea his throne, while sacred Egypt
    Honours his godhead.

The earth, the mother once of godlike Theseus
And mighty Heracles, at length is weary,
And now brings forth a spawn of antlike creatures,
    Blackening her valleys,

Inglorious in their birth and in their living,
Curious and querulous, afraid of battle,
Rummaging earth for coals, in camps of hovels
    Crouching from winter,

As if grim fate, amid our boastful prating,
Made us the image of our brutish fathers,
When from their caves they issued, crazed with terror,
    Howling and hungry.

For all things come about in sacred cycles,
And life brings death, and light eternal darkness,
And now the world grows old apace; its glory
    Passes for ever.

Perchance the earth will yet for many ages
Bear her dead child, her moon, around her orbit;
Strange craft may tempt the ocean streams, new forests
    Cover the mountains.

If in those latter days men still remember
Our wisdom and our travail and our sorrow,
They never can be happy, with that burden
    Heavy upon them,

Knowing the hideous past, the blood, the famine,
The ancestral hate, the eager faith's disaster,
All ending in their little lives, and vulgar
    Circle of troubles.

But if they have forgot us, and the shifting
Of sands has buried deep our thousand cities,
Fell superstition then will seize upon them;
    Protean error,

Will fill their panting heart with sickly phantoms
Of sudden blinding good and monstrous evil;
There will be miracles again, and torment,
        Dungeon, and fagot, —

Until the patient earth, made dry and barren,
Sheds all her herbage in a final winter,
And the gods turn their eyes to some far distant
        Bright constellation.

IV

Slowly the black earth gains upon the yellow,
And the caked hill-side is ribbed soft with furrows.
Turn now again, with voice and staff, my ploughman,
  Guiding thy oxen.

Lift the great ploughshare, clear the stones and
  brambles,
Plant it the deeper, with thy foot upon it,
Uprooting all the flowering weeds that bring not
  Food to thy children.

Patience is good for man and beast, and labour
Hardens to sorrow and the frost of winter.
Turn then again, in the brave hope of harvest,
  Singing to heaven.

V

Of thee the Northman by his beachèd galley
Dreamt, as he watched the never-setting Ursa
And longed for summer and thy light, O sacred
    Mediterranean.

Unseen he loved thee; for the heart within him
Knew earth had gardens where he might be blessed,
Putting away long dreams and aimless, barbarous
    Hunger for battle.

The foretaste of thy langours thawed his bosom;
A great need drove him to thy caverned islands
From the gray, endless reaches of the outer
    Desert of ocean.

He saw thy pillars, saw thy sudden mountains
Wrinkled and stark, and in their crooked gorges,
'Neath peeping pine and cypress, guessed the torrent
    Smothered in flowers.

Thine incense to the sun, thy gathered vapours,
He saw suspended on the flanks of Taurus,
Or veiling the snowed bosom of the virgin
    Sister of Atlas.

He saw the luminous top of wide Olympus,
Fit for the happy gods; he saw the pilgrim
River, with rains of Ethiopia flooding
    Populous Egypt.

And having seen, he loved thee. His racked spirit,
By thy breath tempered and the light that clothes thee,
Forgot the monstrous gods, and made of Nature
    Mistress and mother.

The more should I, O fatal sea, before thee
Of alien words make echoes to thy music;
For I was born where first the rills of Tagus
    Turn to the westward,

And wandering long, alas! have need of drinking
Deep of the patience of thy perfect sadness,
O thou that constant through the change of ages,
    Beautiful ever,

Never wast wholly young and void of sorrows,
Nor ever canst be old, while yet the morning
Kindles thy ripples, or the golden evening
    Dyes thee in purple.

Thee, willing to be tamed but still untamable,
The Roman called his own until he perished,
As now the busy English hover o'er thee,
    Stalwart and noble;

But all is naught to thee, while no harsh winter
Congeals thy fountains, and the blown Sahara
Chokes not with dreadful sand thy deep and placid
    Rock-guarded havens.

Thou carest not what men may tread thy margin;
Nor I, while from some heather-scented headland
I may behold thy beauty, the eternal
    Solace of mortals.

VARIOUS POEMS

EASTER HYMN

I love the pious candle-light,
   The boys' fresh voices, void of thought,
The woman's eager, inward sight
   Of what in vain her heart had sought.

I love the violets at the feet
   Of Jesus, red with some blood-stain;
I love the cross, and it is sweet
   To make a sacrifice of pain.

Some offer bullocks to the skies;
   Some, incense, with their drowsy praise;
He brings the gods what most they prize
   Who sorrow on the altar lays.

I love the Virgin's flowering shrine,
   Her golden crown, her jewelled stole,
The seven dolorous swords that shine
   Around her heart, an aureole.

Thou Mother of a suffering race,
   Whose pangs console us for our birth,
Reign thou for ever, by the grace
   Of sorrow, Queen of all the earth!

Perchance when Carnival is done,
   And sun and moon go out for me,
Christ will be God, and I the one
   That in my youth I used to be.

Things all are shadows, shadows all,
   And ghosts within an idiot's brain.
A little while, they fade and fall;
   A little while, they come again.

Sing softly, choristers; ye sing
  Not faith alone, but doubt and dread.
Ring wildly, Easter bells; ye ring
  For Christ arisen, and hope dead.

GOOD FRIDAY HYMN

I

When the Lord Christ paid life with death,
  Beside the cross his Mother stood;
She saw her Child yield up his breath,
  She knew the passing of her God.

And He said: Lady, though I go,
  I leave thee not without a son;
All men for whom my blood doth flow
  Shall call thee mother, — all for one.

This bitter life is past for me,
  I can thy love no farther prove;
But many eyes shall turn to thee:
  Behold thy son in them I love!

And Mary said: So be it done;
    Be they my children in thy stead;
I will love all, who loved but one,
    And in the living see the dead.

II

My soul's Lord, too, paid life with death,
    And empty was her wide abode;
She saw her child yield up his breath,
    She knew the passing of her God.

And she said: Lord, since thou art gone,
    Thou canst my love no farther prove;
But while I live each flower and stone
    Shall bear thy name and prove my love.

CAPE COD

The low sandy beach and the thin scrub pine,
The wide reach of bay and the long sky line, —
 O, I am sick for home!

The salt, salt smell of the thick sea air,
And the smooth round stones that the ebbtides wear, -
 When will the good ship come?

The wretched stumps all charred and burned,
And the deep soft rut where the cartwheel turned, -
 Why is the world so old?

The lapping wave, and the broad gray sky
Where the cawing rooks and the slow gulls fly,
 Where are the dead untold?

The thin, slant willows by the flooded bog,
The huge stranded hulk and the floating log,
    Sorrow with life began!

And among the dark pines, and along the flat shore,
O the wind, and the wind, for evermore!
    What will become of man?

LENTEN GREETING

TO A LADY

They must find it sweet to pray
Who like you have understood
All the charm of being good,
All the worth of being gay.
By the thought that we are clay,
Is proud grief itself subdued,
May the secret of the Rood
In your sorrow be your stay!
Spring your pleasures will renew,
For the heart is merry after
That to Heaven hath been true;
And, more low for Lenten calm,
Then the music of your laughter
Will have joy as of a psalm.

DECIMA

Silent daisies out of reach,
Maidens of the starry grass,
Gazing on me as I pass
With a look too wise for speech,
Teach me resignation, — teach
Patience to the barren clod,
As, above your happier sod,
Bending to the wind's caress,
You — unplucked, alas! — no less
Sweetly manifest the god.

A TOAST

See this bowl of purple wine,
Life-blood of the lusty vine!
All the warmth of summer suns
In the vintage liquid runs,
All the glow of winter nights
Plays about its jewel lights,
Thoughts of time when love was young
Lurk its ruby drops among,
And its deepest depths are dyed
With delight of friendship tried.
Worthy offering, I ween,
For a god or for a queen,
Is the draught I pour to thee, —
Comfort of all misery,

Single friend of the forlorn,
Haven of all beings born,
Hope when trouble wakes at night,
And when naught delights, delight.
Holy Death, I drink to thee;
Do not part my friends and me.
Take this gift, which for a night
Puts dull leaden care to flight,
Thou who takest grief away
For a night and for a day.

CHORUS

IMMORTAL love,
Whose essence is this pregnant warmth of air,
O hear my prayer,
And tune my fervent hymn as high above
All songs in rapture as thou, sovereign Love,
Art high above the other gods in power.
For whatsoever things on earth are fair
Are thine : thou giv'st the flower
Its colours and its sweet,
And in the foot-prints of thy silent feet
The daisies star the prairie, and the shower
Is thine, that steeps the verdure of the mead ;
By thee the steed
Is beautiful, and every noble breed
By thee remains to ages that succeed ;
For thee the antelope is fleet ;

For thee the hornèd bull is strong to breast
The swollen torrent, bellowing to his herd;
      The painted bird
For thee hath music and to thee addressed,
And the brief sadness of his dying note
Is for thy bitter absence and thy pain;
Thine is the rapture of his swelling throat,
      And thine my strain.
      O fill me once again
With thy lost sweetness now! As a slow wave
Laps the dank hollows of a seaworn cave
In deepest calm, and with prophetic sigh
Repeats the ceaseless rhythm of the storm,
      So let thy pulses warm
      Mine immost soul with high
Hope of the things to be, or wake a vanished form.

LUCIFER

LUCIFER

A PRELUDE

HERMES (*alighting*).

What star art thou, and by what god beguiled
    To wander in this heaven,
    Far from the serene and mild
    Circle of the sisters seven?
O blasted rock, untenanted and wild,
    By lightnings riven,
    Receive thou me,—
O goddess, if the Pleiad lost thou be,
    Lost, too, and driven
By viewless currents of the ethereal sea.
                  (*Kisses the ground.*)
    For Earth, my mother, while her child

    Wings these frozen spaces drear,
    O, how otherwise enisled
    In her blue and liquid sphere
    Swims, forgetting grief, and sleeps
Wrapped in the fleeces of her atmosphere!
    Above Olympus, Phœbe dim,
  Patiently shines the while, and keeps
Still watch in heaven; while below the rim
Of ocean now her brother's steeds uprear
Their fiery manes apace, and dawn is near.
But here no dawn is, and no morning star;
    The suns that nearest are
    Show like a twinkling host, and peer
Through the cold night immeasurably far.

Here who can dwell? If there be deities
Whose body stone, whose spirit silence is,
Here they might slumber frozen. Wrinkled brow
And cloven sides of mountains, heaped up rocks,

Toys of young giants long since dead, and thou,
Horrid abyss, that meteors hot might plough
From heaven falling, and ye vales, by shocks
Of earthquake split in snowy chasms, — O, speak,
If ye have tongues or any shadowy life!
    The stranger do not wrong, —
    A god, though seeming weak,
Who prays you, with the winds too long at strife,
For shelter from this night and stinging thong
Of sleet. O, answer me, if any banished soul
Haunts you, and guards from harm the frozen pole.

    LUCIFER (*advancing*).
Nay, not a banished soul! — What seems forlorn,
Hermes, to thee, another loveth best;
    In this crag, the throne of scorn,
    Hath a bolder spirit rest.

    HERMES.
Thou who callest me by name,
Large spectre plumèd for the eagle's flight,

> Let me be thy guest this night,
> If kindness move thy breast, or any flame
> Leap on thy hearth, that henceforth, ever bright,
> > On this hoarse and angry coast
> May gleam the beacon of its sacred light,
> > Where a god, by fortune hurled,
> > Found an altar and a host
> High on the utmost headland of the world.

LUCIFER.

> Stranger, look upon this face;
> Look long, nor let thy fond heart rashly speak.
> Seest thou mortal blood within this cheek?
> > Do not think thy brothers' grace
> Befits all spirits: some there be too high
> > To wear outward glory still;
> > For it passes nature's skill
> > To paint reason to the eye,
> Or cast in mould indomitable will.
> > My hand drew yon starry girth

About the middle of the hollow sky;
　　I have stood a witness by
　　At the founding of the earth;
　　I have seen the twelve gods' birth,
Alas! and I await to see them die.

　　　　　HERMES.
Imperious spirit, I would not offend.
　　Thy heart knows if this be truth,
And mine eyes, on thee gazing, comprehend
　　That thou art a god in sooth.
　　Be then gracious, and befriend
The stranger, and beside thee grant me rest,
That I gain strength unto my journey's end,
And see again Olympus' gleaming crest
　　And the brothers that I love.

　　　　　LUCIFER.
　　But what error brought the dove
　　To the eagle's wintry nest?

HERMES.
I wandered long upon an idle quest,
And found no other isle in all the deep.

LUCIFER.
    Luckless for the child of Jove
To set his wingèd foot upon this steep.
No vines upon so wild a ruin creep;
No Nereid bathes in such an icy cove.
But, come; there is a cavern in the hill.

HERMES.
'T will be a covert from this piercing air.

LUCIFER.
My servant's fire shall medicine thy chill.
This way; 't is dark along the icy stair.
                (*Gives Hermes his hand.*)

HERMES.
Art thou a serpent, that thy flesh is cold?

LUCIFER.

They call me so. My blood was hot of old.

HERMES.

But froze from breathing long this cruel storm?

LUCIFER.

Nay, my good Hermes, it was not the wind,
Which only bites because the heart is warm;
Mine cannot suffer. In my youth I sinned,
And loved the soft caresses of the world.
Now I am free. I have forsworn delight,
Which makes us slaves.

HERMES.

            The chill of wintry night
Keeps germs from budding; with no leaf unfurled,
Dies the imprisoned deity within.
How, then, shouldst thou be free beneath the blight
Of this sharp flaw?

LUCIFER.

          I can be free from sin. —
                    (*They reach the cave.*)
Lyal! Ho, Lyal! — Sleeping by the fire?
Waken the embers, boy; pile drift-wood up,
That we have light and comfort while we sup.
And bring my cloak, — if that such coarse attire
Can please thee, being warm, on such a night. —
          (*To Hermes. They sit down and eat.*)
Guests come not often hither, for the sky
Grudges me chance of hospitality,
Lest that small virtue in me wound its sight.

HERMES.

But is the sky thine enemy?

LUCIFER.

                  Thou seest
It doth not flatter: yet 't is the ally
Of one that wrongs us both.

HERMES.

                Why, if thou fleest
Into the whirlwind, on thee it must blow.

LUCIFER.

Ah, if thou knewest!

HERMES.

Art thou here confined?

LUCIFER.

By a great sorrow and a tameless mind.

HERMES.

A sorrow?

LUCIFER.

Listen, if thou needs must know.
There is among the stars one greatest star
Which showeth dark, and none may see it shine.
Men know it by their hope; a hand divine
Must darkly lead them thither from afar.
But once within its bounds, eternal light
Streams on their ampler souls, and there they are
What upon earth they would be. Of this realm
An ancient God is king, majestic, wise,
Of triple form, and all-beholding eyes.

The terror of his glance can overwhelm
The sense, as lightning when it rends the skies.
The dread words of his mouth are gladly heard,
But marvellous their meaning, not to prove
Except by faith and argument of love.
He saith he fashioned nature with a word,
And in him all things are and live and move.
To that fair kingdom from primeval night
I passed; and, clad in splendour and in might,
I led the armies of my father, God.
My right hand urged them with a sword of light;
My left hand ruled them with a flowering rod.
Brave was my youth, and pleasing in his sight,—
Next him in honour; till one day, discourse
Upon his greatness and our being's source
Led me to question: "Tell, O Lord, the cause
Why sluggish nature doth with thee contend,
And thy designs, observant of her laws,
By tortuous paths must struggle to their end."
To this, with many words of little pith,

He answered.
And as when sailors, crossing some broad frith,
Spy in the lurid west a sudden gloom
And grasp the rudder, taking double reef,
I nerved my heart for battle; for my doom
I saw upon me, and that I was born
To suffer, and to fill the world with grief.
But strong in reason, terrible in scorn,
I rose. "Seek not, O Lord, my King," I cried,
"With solemn phrases to deceive my doubt.
Tell me thy thought, or I will pluck it out
With bitter question. Make thy prudent choice!
Either confess that how thou cam'st to be,
Or why the winds are docile to thy voice,
And why the will to make us was in thee,
And why the partners of thy life are three,
Thou canst not know, but even as the rest
That wake to life behold the sun and moon,
And feel their natural passions stir their breast,
They know not why, so thou from some long swoon

Awaking once, didst with supreme surprise
Scan thy deep bosom and the vault of heaven, —
For I did so, when fate unsealed mine eyes
(Thy small zeal for the truth shall be forgiven
If thou confess it now, and I will still
Call thee my master, for thou rulest well,
And in thy kingdom I have loved to dwell) ; —
Or else, if truth offend thy pampered will,
And with caressing words and priestly spell
Thou wouldst seduce me, henceforth I rebel."
I knew his answer, and I drew my sword,
And many spirits gathered to my side.
But in high heaven he is still the Lord;
I am an exile in these spaces wide
Where none is master. The north wind and the west
Are my companions, and the void my rest.

HERMES.

'T is much. When evil fortune bows a friend,
We blush that we are happy.

LUCIFER.

    Nay, rejoice!
The pleasant music of a tempered voice
Is cure for sadness. If my grief could end,
It would, with dreaming of an age of gold
When all were blessed.

HERMES.

    They who serve thy King,
Are they not blessed still?

LUCIFER.

    A doubtful thing
Is blessedness like that. They grow not old,
They live in friendship, and their wondering eyes,
Blinded to nature, feed on fantasies.
Their raptured souls, like lilies in a stream,
That from their fluid pillow never rise,
Float on the lazy current of a dream.
My grief is not that I am not like them,

Or that the splendour of my life is less.
My soul hath kinship with the wilderness.
But rage that fate should ever overwhelm
The right with cunning and the truth with lies,
And that the lust of living never dies,
Gnaws at my heart; my noble trust deceived
In reason's might and in the power of truth,
The unthought-of shame that I should stand alone
When universal nature was aggrieved
And should have mutinied! Faith of my youth,
That my stout heart did never yet disown,
Prove thyself true, and still to be believed!
Hasten, just day, and hurl him from his throne,
As children in a chasm cast a stone!

HERMES.

That day may come, but wishing now is vain.
Rest from this passion. Much I fear my speech
Hath stirred unwittingly a slumbering pain.
Let it not tarry after, I beseech,
But now fly with me from thy thoughts again.

LUCIFER.

Thou goest? — Thy way lies straight athwart the main.
From that bright planet thou wilt see two suns.
The farther one is thine; thence easy runs
Thy course. Thou camest far for little gain.

HERMES.

Not so. Acquaintance with so high a mind
Rewards me for my journey. Let not space,
To whose dimensions mortals are confined,
Sever two gods; but let us face to face
Meet in some desert, hallowing the place.
It is not well for thee to dwell apart
On this bleak mountain; if thy wound is deep,
To natural slumber yield thy tortured heart.
Watch not these feeble stars, sad lamps of grief,
But close thine eyes on the vain past, and sleep.

LUCIFER.

Sleep? — yet why not? When every shivering
    leaf

From the proud oak is stripped by autumn's flaw,
He suffers winter's deep, oblivious snows
To choke his anguish and enshroud his woes,
Nor wakes till the new buds begin to thaw
And the whole forest is alive with song.
Yes, sleep ! The child, rebellious at some wrong,
Frets in his helpless pain till nature dries,
Closing his smarting eyelids, his dim eyes ;
They open merry in the morning light ;
Then his keen pang is nothing, and his cries
The all-forgotten dream of yesternight.
But is my grief a child's ? Am I so slight ?
Or could my bosom, like the wanton trees,
Put forth its blooms to any wind that blew ?
Say that it could ; say that some vernal breeze
Melted my winter ; could my vain forgetting
Make Heaven just, or make the past not true ?
The evil lives, and if I ceased regretting,
I should be more unhappy than I knew.

HERMES.

No one is truly happy. Evil things
Fate lays upon us; yet she makes amends,
Bringing us daily comfort on the wings
Of sleep, and by the willing hands of friends.

LUCIFER.

Of friends?

HERMES.

Thou hadst none? Deem that time is far.
Friendship is knitted in a single night
'Twixt noble minds. Quench not the memory quite,
If I to-day was welcome in this star;
But let that breed new kindness. I in turn
Would greet you in my kingdom; it is fair.
The wisest mind hath something still to learn,
And I might teach oblivion to thee there.
Soon let me meet thee, as I scud the air
At evening, where the outer planets burn.
But now, farewell. *(He flies away.)*

LUCIFER.

Farewell. Is this a dream?
What vital breath is blowing on my soul?
Into my deepest bosom falls a gleam
That makes me wish to live. O, strange! I seem
As if escaping from mine own control,
As if a fever waned, and opiate balm
Were running through my veins. The gates of hell
Are open to the morning and the spell
Of the chill dewy glades. They waft such calm
As heaven's garden knew when evening fell
In gold and purple, and each conscious flower
Blessed God, and inly felt his brother sing
Inaudibly the praises of the spring.
Lyal!

LYAL.

My Lord.

LUCIFER.

Nothing exceeds the power
Of time and nature. 'T were a wondrous thing

If once again the womb of ancient night
Were big with being, and a giant came,
A rival to the other! O, the fight,
The victory, the fallen tyrant's shame!
Lyal!

              LYAL.

    My Lord.

             LUCIFER.

              He hath a wondrous charm,
A gentle hand, warm, made to touch a friend's;
A well-born, open spirit, that attends
To others' words; a young god's strength of arm;
The inward smile of them that know no harm.
Lyal!

              LYAL.

    My Lord.

             LUCIFER.

          There should be no more pain,
And I in that republic of the just

Might live from day to day in peace, and trust
That life, although mysterious, was not vain.
Ho, Lyal, hear'st thou not?

LYAL.

My Lord, I hear,
But do not understand your sacred words.

LUCIFER.

What should now be the season of the year?

LYAL.

Methinks it should be spring.

LUCIFER.

Canst hear the birds!

LYAL.

Birds in this island, without sedge or tree?

LUCIFER.

They now are singing in my memory.
How weary must these watches be for thee,
Serving me here! Thou art too young a boy
To languish in this desert.

LYAL.

'T is my joy,
My Lord, to serve you, wheresoe'er it be.

LUCIFER.

We must away; this night shall have its dreams.
Thou shalt behold a green land, watered well,
Where large white swans swim in the lucent streams;
And bosky thickets where the harpy screams;
And centaurs scouring fields of asphodel,
While young fauns pluck their beards, and start away
At great Pan's feast to pipe an interlude.
There mermaids with the painted dolphins play,
Splashing blue waves for rainbows in the spray;

And friendly poets, straying through the wood,
Lay finger to the mouth, to watch askance
How in wild ring the nymphs and satyrs dance.
Wouldst thou not go?

    LYAL.

      'T is as my Master wills.

    LUCIFER.
Ay, ay, make ready! —
      Sad, familiar hills,
For how long do I leave you? Not for ever;
A voice of inward warning tells me so.
Forget ye not my voice; your silence fills
My bosom always; no, I cannot sever
The bond that binds me to your sunless snow.
But farewell for a season. Far I go,
Far, though I know not whither; for the breath
Of life is on me — or the hand of death.
      (*They fly away.*)

ImTheStory.com

Personalized Classic Books in many genre's

Unique gift for kids, partners, friends, colleagues

Customize:

- Character Names
- Upload your own front/back cover images (optional)
- Inscribe a personal message/dedication on the inside page (optional)

Customize many titles Including
- Alice in Wonderland
- Romeo and Juliet
- The Wizard of Oz
- A Christmas Carol
- Dracula
- Dr. Jekyll & Mr. Hyde
- And more...

Printed by BoD™in Norderstedt, Germany